Surprising Insects Magazine
Masters of Disguise

by Amanda Adams

PEARSON
Scott Foresman

Editorial Offices: Glenview, Illinois • Parsippany, New Jersey • New York, New York
Sales Offices: Needham, Massachusetts • Duluth, Georgia • Glenview, Illinois
Coppell, Texas • Sacramento, California • Mesa, Arizona

Introduction

Hello, readers of *Surprising Insects Magazine!* In this issue, we will look at insects as masters of disguise. We think you are going to like what you see—or what you don't see!

In "Surprise, Surprise!" we will show you some insects that look like other insects or creatures. We will also show some insects that do not look like insects at all.

On page 7, you will learn about two different kinds of butterflies that look alike in "Royal Confusion."

You will read a poem (page 8) about a common insect that is a master of disguise. You might even want to write a poem after you see how beautiful all of these insects are!

Happy reading, and get ready to see some amazing bugs!

Do you see big, scary eyes on this emperor moth? Many creatures do, and they stay away from the moth. But the scary eyes really are large, false eye spots on the moth's wings.

Surprise, Surprise!

For more than 300 million years, scientists say, insects have survived because they have adapted in certain ways. One of these ways is to look like something different than what they really are.

Insects do not do this on purpose. The way they look is a result of how insects adapted to survive. Science indicates that those insects survived because of how they looked. Their looks have helped them escape being eaten or helped them catch food to eat.

Syrphid flies are harmless, but they look like wasps and bees. This keeps some predators from attacking them.

Here are some of the adaptations that help insects survive.

Some insects *mimic,* or imitate, other insects or creatures. If a harmless insect looks like a harmful insect or creature, predators stay away. Result: The insect escapes being eaten, and so it survives.

This works the other way, too. A harmful insect can look like a harmless one and surprise its prey. Result: The harmful insect gets to eat, and so it survives.

---

predators: animals that kill and eat other animals for food
prey: animal that is taken and eaten

Can you see the camouflaged African praying mantis?

Some insects have coloring or patterns that enable them to blend into a background. This is called *camouflage* (KAM uh flahzh). It helps an insect to look like other things around it. That way it is hard for other insects or creatures to see the insect. You must look very carefully to find a camouflaged insect. A camouflaged insect seems to be almost invisible.

Camouflage can be helpful in two ways. A camouflaged predator can surprise the insect that it is hunting for food. Or a camouflaged prey becomes almost invisible, and its predator will not see it and attack it.

---

invisible: not able to be seen

This walking stick insect is well hidden among twigs and branches.

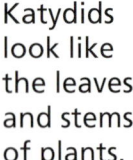

Katydids look like the leaves and stems of plants.

Some insects look like other things in nature, such as twigs or leaves. This appearance is called a *disguise*. For a disguise to work, the insect stays very still for hours at a time.

You can see above two insects on this page that survive because they look like something else around them. There are many more insects that have such adaptations. Some insects look like dead leaves, tree bark, beautiful flowers, or something else in nature. These disguises are critical to their survival.

Royal Confusion

This is an article about two different kinds of butterflies that look very much alike: the Monarch butterfly and the Viceroy butterfly.

Monarch butterfly

Viceroy butterfly

These butterflies have orange, black, and white wings. You can tell them apart because the Viceroy has a thin stripe going across its bottom wings.

Both kinds of butterflies are poisonous to birds and other predators. Some scientists believe that looking so much alike helps both species. Predators stay away from all kinds of orange, black, and white butterflies, even if they have tried to eat only one kind!

Extend Language — **Royal Titles for Butterflies**

Monarch is another word for *king* or *queen*. The word *viceroy* means "a person who rules a land, acting in place of a king or queen." The prefix *vice-* means "taking the place of" or "instead of." The pictures show why *Viceroy* is the name of a butterfly that looks like it can take the place of a Monarch butterfly.

Leafhopper

You are as green as the leaf that is your home,
Green as the stem you crawl upon,
Green as the grass on which you roam.

Tiny creature, my delight,
Landing on my skin so light,
Gently tickling as you go.
You know all you need to know.
Stay a moment, fill my eyes
With your clever green disguise.
Make me wish that I were green.
Make me wish I were unseen
Against leaf and stem and grass,
Blending with all that I pass.

---
roam: wander, move about